Copyright © 2021
KIMI KANE

All rights reserved. No part of this publication may be reproduced, distributed, or transmitted in any form or by any means, including photocopying, recording, or other electronic or mechanical methods, without the prior written permission of the publisher, except in the case of brief quotations embodied in critical reviews and certain other noncommercial uses permitted by copyright law.

INTRODUCTION

We all know Roberto Firmino. Throughout his career, the superstar dazzled us with pinpoint passing, the ability to hold the ball and run rings around his opponents, and the creative and sometimes unorthodox assists that resulted in iconic and truly beautiful goals.

But who is Firmino? Where did he come from, what kind of childhood did he have, and who helped him reach this fame and success level?

This is a list of all the questions that we will answer in *this book. Along the way, we'll explore the life of one of football's* most eccentric and beloved stars, and we'll learn about his family and his home town.

Are you interested in learning how an ordinary man in Liverpool was able to rise to the level of fame he is at today, and what events transpired in his life for this to be possible?

It seems that the referee is blowing his whistle, so it's time to start.

EARLY CHILDHOOD

Let's start from the beginning, and by doing this, we will get to meet Roberto Firmino's family.

Roberto Firmino Barbosa de Oliveira, his full name but probably too long to put on the back of a jersey, was born on October 2nd, 1991. His hometown is called Maceio Alagoas, which is located in Brazil. Every Firmino fan knows he's Brazilian. But we guess you already knew that. His father is named José Roberto Cordeiro, and his mother goes by the name of Mariana Cícera Barbosa de Oliveira.

José Roberto Cordeiro has 12 siblings. The youngest, José Roberto, is his namesake. After being born in Angola, the family fled to Mozambique for safety only to be caught in the crossfire of civil war. They managed to escape to Brazil, where they spent their childhood years in poverty.

Roberto's parents' jobs were to protect their son from everything going on around them, but they did a good job of keeping him safe. Roberto grew up in a rough part of Maceio and had a tough childhood, but he could still find the love he needed from his family. The gangs and street crimes that occurred by night were not suitable for a little boy who had nothing to do with the terrible things happening all over the neighbourhood. They had a chilling effect on his psyche, and he couldn't enjoy his time in this world.

His mother ever said that she was so scared and worried for her son's life that she even went as far as to forbid him from leaving the house as a child, having one thing on her mind. Her young son would be impressionable enough to be persuaded by the others and ultimately get involved in the activities that terrorized the area, ultimately joining one of the gangs. She wouldn't have any of that, so as the caring mother that she was, and still is, she did everything in her power to prevent such a thing from happening.

As quoted, his mother revealed the following: "I didn't want Roberto to go out and play because it was very dangerous on the streets."

The only way young Roberto was allowed to leave the house was in the presence of his father. The two would leave every day, José having a water business, and show his son the ropes. Being his own business, the father of the future football superstar hoped that one day he could expand the business and make it a true source of income for his family (at that moment in time, he was only making enough to pay for their daily needs). His son would be a little older, and he would carry on the tradition and take over the "family business." But how wrong he was, we might add.

Roberto had one thing on his mind: football. He didn't care about water, and he didn't see that his family struggled. The only image that would occupy his mind was the image of a football. This was his passion; this was his true fire.

Even though young Roberto was not allowed to leave the house on his own, thus the only way he could do it was inside the house.

Still, his mother, of course, would not allow it, the young dreamer, being a crafty individual, managed to find a way to do the thing he loved most.

When the moment came, Roberto would quietly get back into the yard, lock the door and sneak into the house without making any noise. He would sneak out of the house and, by using his own special key that he managed to get his hands on, would unlock the fence door and would play for hours and hours. He would do so until it was time for his mother to wake up.

It was later reported that his mother would say, "He would get up really early while I was sleeping to play football. He used to make as little noise as possible while having his own key which I didn't know about."

Roberto Firmino had a rough childhood, but this only made him the man he is today. His parents knew that keeping him locked inside was not an option. What kind of opportunities could he have if he didn't leave the safety of his own home?

So, at age 8, his parents decided that would change their entire family's life forever.

They decided to let him play football in the streets, but why this sudden change of heart?

The two would hear daily that their son is truly talented. Each early morning, he would sneak out to play, some neighbours would see him, and by being impressed by the young boy's talent and his level of skill, they would talk to his parents, praising their son.

These praises made them rethink their strategy of keeping him safe.

During an interview with Roberto Firmino's mother, she stated the following: "He would always fall asleep hugging his football after every match."

Today's superstar had to overcome a tough upbringing to succeed in life. He learned the hardships of a tough life at an early age when he would borrow money to get to football training, but he was proud and didn't like the act of borrowing money at all. However, it was his only option if he wanted to keep playing.

THE START OF SOMETHING MAGICAL

The CRB where Roberto Firmino started to make a name for himself at a very young age of 14. The name of the coach that kept Roberto Firmino on the right track was Luiz. He was the coach at their local club.

As his former coach, Luiz, stated: "Roberto's family was very poor and humble. When he first came to the club, his father was unemployed. He only managed his small business to feed his family, so I paid for Roberto's travel expenses, helped him with his kit, and took him to games. He would play in his bare feet. He was an intimidating, tall young man who was quiet most of the time, but he was very street smart. I knew that he had never been drawn into drug trafficking or other crimes like stealing a car.

His coach saw it the very moment he touched the ball. It was something about his game and about his passion, never thinking of giving up and always finding ways out from tricky situations. He had something special.

Coach Luiz continued: "Within the first few minutes of him being on the field, I knew he was going to be a star. I cried when I heard he had been called to play for Brazil. I felt so proud of him, to see that he has fulfilled what I dreamed of and what he dreamed of. He always told me that his dream was to become one of Brazil's best footballers.

For the next two years, Firmino trained, and he did so with an intensity that you don't see very often. He was a talent, this thing was clear, but as we all know, hard work beats talent every day of the week.

At 16, Roberto was sent on loan to a Brazilian second-division side called Figueirense.

From his mom, we found out that her son was homesick. It was the first time he'd been so far from home, and club life wasn't always easy. Even though he was talented, he played with better players than he did before, so he had to put in even more work to stand out amongst them.

But let's explore how he came to join the club.

There are good game trials, excellent game trials, and game trials like Roberto Firmino had in 2007 at Figueirense.

The 16-year-old had travelled more than 3,000 kilometres along the east coast of Brazil, accompanied by dental surgeon Marcellus Portella. He was part of the medical team of the Brazilian second league CRB club when he first saw Firmino playing for one of the junior teams. Impressed by the young man's evolution, Portella immediately offered to become his representative. The plan was for Firmino to earn enough money to lift his family out of the poverty in which he lived and provide a better life for his family. The Brazilian soccer manager, Portella, connected Toninho Almieida - the youth coach for CRB - with Luciano "Bilu" Lopes - a veteran soccer player from Atletico Mineiro. Bilu originally grew up in Maceió.

Bilu helped organize two-game trials in Sao Paulo and Figueirense in the Brazilian league, with the first resulting in a failure and the second proving to be a success. Sports director Erasmo Damiani remembers the moment with a smile on his face. "It was my decision, one of which I will never regret," he said. "In the first half-hour of this morning's training, Roberto scored two goals. Hemerson Maia, the U17 coach, came in a hurry to the office insisting that we not lose him."

The same thing happened in the afternoon with the U20 coach, Rogerio Micale. "If Hemerson doesn't take him, I want the kid on my team." Roberto was so talented that Firmino received the contract right then, Figueirense was in full campaign preparation for its 2008 season. In January through May, he would take part in the Campeonato Catarinense, a regional level of Santa Catarina, and then follow the Serie A season.

From an interview taken a few years ago, his mother said the following: "He called me many times desperate to come home. 'Mum, come and get me. I can't take this anymore!' The entire family wanted to bring him home, but we couldn't afford it."

Despite being an aspiring actor, the future star's only option was to wait patiently for a couple of months to earn enough money so he could come back home and visit his family.

While he was at the club, he was focused. He knew what he had to do. His dream was to make it big and take his family out of poverty. He wanted fame and recognition so badly that the thought of it fueled him and gave him hope for a better future. His family went from living in poverty to providing for themselves with a little bit of extra income from his soccer skills.

The only road that would lead to all of his dreams becoming a reality was filled with hard work, sacrifices, and discipline. Firmino wanted a miracle but, just how good things come to those who work hard for them, the miracle appeared in our young prospect's life.

THE BIG LEAGUE

As we said before, hard work pays off, and it certainly did for Roberto Firmino. The raw talent he had, combined with an unbreakable will to escape the financial status his family was in, and hours upon hours of training, made the player noticeable.

During this time, the German goalkeeper Lutz Pfannenstiel arrived in Brazil. Having played in leagues worldwide, such as New Zealand, Norway, and South Africa, he had extensive experience and knowledge of different styles of play. He was moments away from signing a six-month contract in Canada, but then he got a phone call. His agent told him there was an offer for him in South America. He said it would be very special for me to add to my list of countries from the five different FIFA confederations.

I took on the challenge, and it turned out to be an unforgettable experience. I had always dreamed of playing in Brazil, so in a few weeks, I signed with Atletico Ibirama, from Santa Catarina. Firmino was in the youth team of Figueirense, a club that was part of our league. "

Pfannestiel never had Firmino as a direct opponent, but the program allowed him to see him in action. The playing conditions, however, were not the most favourable to highlight the young man's talent. "The youth teams often played on the same weekend with the first team, so I was lucky to see young Roberto a few times. However, that league had little in common with what you would imagine about Brazilian football. It was a harsh, physically-based southern environment; don't think about samba-inspired football. It was about long balls and opponents who didn't miss a chance to hurt you. "

His magic while he had the ball and his high IQ when it came to positioning, as well as the stats he gathered. At the same time, he played for the Brazilian club, which made him stand out.

This harsh environment gave Firmino, in time, extra resistance. Off the field, however, he was a character of extreme shyness. Damiani remembers amusedly, "If you went and told him he wouldn't get his salary that month, he would look at you and smile. It was incredible. He was so shy that people asked me if he was dumb. "But shyness could not hide his talent. "Arsenal had targeted him and those there were thinking of making an offer.

PSV was also interested, coming with the promise of an official invitation, but everything took too long ", reveals Damiani. The first team to come up with a concrete offer was Marseille in the summer of 2009. Their invitation to a game trial also included a plane ticket to Paris, so for the 17-year-old, there was an excellent opportunity to enter European football. But everything would fall apart on Spanish soil. His flight to France stopped in Madrid at Barajas Airport, the bridge between South America and Europe, well known for its strict immigration procedures.

All documents were checked on Firmino. He was interrogated and then taken to a room with other disoriented passengers, informed that their journey ended there. The first available flight took Roberto back to Brazil. "It was a traumatic experience for him," Damiani explains. "In Madrid, he was asked for all kinds of documents that he did not have. He was desperate, alone, and did not speak Spanish at all. He called his parents at the airport in tears."

"I talked to a police officer in Madrid and sent him a fax specifying the period of time he was to train with Marseille, but at that time there were some unresolved diplomatic tensions between Brazil and Spain, so they simply deported him."

And if that wasn't enough, anyone going through this process would be banned from entering Spain for the next ten years. Fortunately, Marseille was determined to see Firmino.

"A month later, they sent him a new invitation, but this time with a non-stop flight, directly to Paris." Another chance for the young Brazilian, another round of training. A new disappointment would follow. "He gave it all for Marseille, but in the end, the French club did not agree to pay the termination clause," says

Damiani disappointed. And Firmino returned to Brazil in tears.

At the end of 2009, a few weeks after reaching the age of majority, Firmino switched to the senior group. Figueirense had been relegated to the second division, but the environment was more conducive to his talent.

In 2010, in his first full season on the big team, Firmino scored eight goals in the league, helping to promote back to Serie A. "Once promoted to the first team, it didn't take long for him to stand out. That season was called the revelation of Serie B ", Damiani recalls. That's when it came to the attention of Ernst Tanner, then sporting director at Hoffenheim.

But the Bundesliga club employee needed more to be fully convinced. "The first time I heard Roberto's name was when a scouting agency in Brazil offered it to us, sending us videos and presenting it in laudatory terms. But at that time, the opinion about the Brazilian players was not very good at Hoffenheim. Carlos Eduardo and Luiz Gustavo had been decent, but everyone else we were offered turned out to be thorns.

"Then Pfannenstiel, the globe-trotter goalkeeper, intervened in the landscape, who was to receive a scout position in Tanner's team. Before starting, the club asked him if he had crossed paths with Firmino in Brazil. "I told them that I had seen him and that he had a huge talent, but that he would have to develop physically to be successful in Germany," Pfannenstiel continues. "Then Ernst decided to go see him in person."

In the fall of 2010, Tanner flew to Brazil. It came when it could not be worse, the competitive calendar being turned upside down by the recently concluded World Cup in South Africa.

The matches originally scheduled for June and July had been postponed, with clubs having to recover during the year, most of the time after tiring trips. "I went to see a match of Figueirense in Goiania, 1200 kilometres from Florianopolis," says Tanner. "It was a long and difficult journey to nowhere. They lost 3-1, Firmino only played the last 27 minutes, and I'm not even sure he touched the ball. "Figueirense returned home and will play again in three days.

With no guarantee that Firmino would play more, Tanner decided to pursue a team training session. It's just that this turned out not to be so easy to do. "I went to the stadium, and they wouldn't let me in. However, I hadn't travelled that far in vain, so I bribed one of the guards. I told him that I was a tourist and that I just wanted to see what the inside of the stadium looked like. In the end, he let me in. "Any trace of frustration disappeared when he saw Firmino. "He was so fast, and he had balance, he hit his head well, he did the defensive phase. In one training session, I saw what I wanted. I was convinced we had to take it. "The scout was certain.

But suppose Tanner was impressed by the striker's qualities. In that case, the same could not be said about Marcio Goiano, the manager of Figueirense. Tanner smiles as he remembers those moments. "Firmino was the most criticized player in the whole group. The other players simply sat and watched as the coach was only talking and criticizing him. Nothing seemed to be right."

Years later, when they both worked for Red Bull - Tanner in Salzburg and Goiano in Bragantino - Tanner asked his colleague why he was so tough that day. "He replied that it was his duty for Firmino to reach his potential, and then he asked me how in the world did I manage to see the training if it was behind closed doors," says Tanner, laughing.

Firmino's attitude meant a lot to Tanner, helping him convince himself of the potential added value the young man would bring to Hoffenheim.

"After such a treatment, many young people would have left the training ground, but Firmino didn't budge. I liked this." And that's not all that impressed him. "At a club like Hoffenheim, you need a number 10 capable of doing both phases. You need someone with the attributes of a game leader but who is willing to also work on the defensive phase. Brazilians are always brilliant with the ball at their feet, but they are rarely willing to defend themselves. Firmino was different." Hoffenheim moved quickly, agreeing to pay the € 4 million termination clause.

"One of the conditions was for Firmino to receive a signing bonus," Tanner said. "He wanted to buy a family home because the area where they lived was so dangerous that we couldn't visit him there."

It was a scary thought to move all the way across the world, to Europe, Germany. It would be a huge cultural shift, but this is what dreams are made of.

He was only 18, but Roberto already made the life of his family better. As soon as he got the news, he thought to himself: "My family will never have to work again."

He made it, but he needed to continue this path of success by implementing the same work ethic he adopted while playing for the Brazilian club.

Finally, the entire family got out of the slum. They exceeded their financial status, all thanks to this young and hungry footballer.

While at Hoffenheim, Roberto became developing his own persona apart from the quality that he brought on the pitch. His personality was huge; from how he conducted himself to his clothing style and haircuts, he truly was different. But more on that later in the book.

FAMILY LIFE

The young talented player was the apple of his parent's eyes. Mariana Cícera Barbosa de Oliveira and José Roberto Cordeiro are the people that raised such a strong, confident and passionate young man. As Roberto often said, he owes everything to his parents because even though they were struggling financially, they did everything they could so that his dream wouldn't die.

To show her support, his mother, Mariana, dressed up by wearing his son's shirt for the national Brazil football team and went to church on an early Sunday morning. Everyone gave her funny looks, but she didn't care. She supported her son before his first-ever national game, and that's what mattered, not what other people thought of her.

After church, she went back home to catch the game on TV. Her son made his debut by entering the pitch in the second half. Her heart was pounding; she was so proud and scared at the same time. Her son was on TV, and he was representing their country. Mariana couldn't believe it.

The entire family was celebrating, and his mother started crying with joy. It was November 2014 when the ultimate reward came for Firmino: the first match and the first goal for the Brazilian national team, scoring in Austria the winning goal at the end of the match.

After the game, he and his mom spoke on the phone. He asked his mother why she was crying, and all she could say was: *"Son, you're too much."*

She knew right then and there that her son was a superstar and would be a great addition to any club worldwide, especially to Brazil's national team.

From that moment on, she started organizing playing sessions for her son and the team each time they would have a match.

In an interview with Brazil's SporTV News channel, she proudly admitted that the world hadn't seen anything yet. Everyone should be prepared for what her son will certainly achieve.

RELATIONSHIP LIFE

With all the success of monetary achievements and his football career, it was the natural step Firmino should take. A talented player of his calibre and such a successful person must have a partner and equally talented and successful wife to balance each other's good and not so good traits.

Here Brazilian model Larissa Pereira enters the scene. She is the girl that stole Firmino's heart and never gave it back. The two met at a popular Brazilian nightclub around the year 2013. It was love at first sight. They quickly hit it off and fell madly in love with each other, announcing their relationship to the public by posting their first pictures together on social media for the entire world to see. The pics were of them working out, wearing matching outfits and looking like the perfect couple all around.

The first coach to work with Roberto, Luiz Guilherme Gomes de Farias, told the Sun in an interview that: "Roberto is just as well known in

Brazil for his fashion sense as he is for what he's done on the pitch and also for his beautiful wife." *The people of Liverpool will love him. He and his wife shine and stand out everywhere they go."*

The cute couple tied the knot in 2015 while still being madly in love. This happened not long before Firmino arrived at Liverpool, but the wedding took place in his hometown of Maceio, Brazil.

Larissa wanted to let her fans know how much she loves and appreciates them for all their support. Her message touched on the man she is lucky enough to be marrying and how he completes her with heartfelt sincerity. She writes, "I chose you and would choose you a thousand times over."

Even though the wedding took place in his hometown, some Liverpool teammates he became close friends with flew to Brazil and attended the wedding. Big names like Philippe Coutinho, Lucas Leiva and Allan Souza were witnesses to the wonderful event. Even more so, Coutinho was named the best man at the wedding. He and Roberto were very good friends, playing at Liverpool and for the national team of Brazil.

After the beautiful couple said their vows and put rings on each other's fingers, the party continued with a special guest in the form of Gabriel Diniz, the famous Brazilian pop star. Guest had a blast, almost all of them snapping pictures and recording videos of the event before posting it on social media.

As a way to give back, Frimino and his new wife, Larissa, asked the guests to go to a dedicated website from where they could buy presents for the newlyweds. Still, the guests could donate as much as they would like for a charitable cause instead of doing that. A two-year-old named Miguel Enrique from Santa Catarina was suffering from a digestive disease. Still, thanks to the donations, his condition improved.

Not long after, the couple was blessed with the greatest gift of all: their first child, a beautiful baby girl named Valentina Firmino. But the blessings didn't stop there for the Firmino family, as not long after, another girl would come into the world. The two named her Bella, a fitting name for a beautiful daughter.

ART LOVER

We talked about how Roberto Firmino had his breakthrough in football. How he did in his first international game, and what was his mother's reaction. He had to work hard to everything he achieved, and he had to stay focused, so he did. Then we discussed his family life and even who was the best man at his wedding. But we are here to know Roberto Firmino even better than that.

Did you know that he loves art? And by art, we mean tattoos, of course. We all know he has tons of them, but what do they mean? What was the concept behind each and every one of his tattoos? Let's dig deep and find out.

Roberto loves to get ink on his skin. The majority of his tattoos are close to his beliefs or are a homage to his family.

While playing for Hoffenheim in Germany, Firmino decided to get a tattoo but not in Portuguese. That is his native language, but in

German. The tattoo says: "Family, never-ending love".

The second tattoo we are going to talk about is in Greek. Yes, we know, from German to Greek, that's quite of a big leap. We don't really know why the football star got a tattoo in Greek, but what we do know is that it means: "God is faithful, " indicating that he is well in tune with his belief in God.

After the birth of his first daughter, Roberto decided to tattoo her name on his chest so that she would always be close to him, no matter where he was in the world. It says Valentina Firmino.

The entirety of his right arm is covered in tattoos as well. But these are not without meaning. The tattoo artist managed to create amazingly realistic portraits of his family members, so he could have them close to him no matter how far away he would be. The tattoos were so good that you couldn't tell if they were real or not!

On the same arm, he had done a red rose which represents love, love for his wife Larissa, a four-leaf clover that represents luck (he considers himself truly lucky to be in the position that he is right now when it comes to his finances, his career or his family), a peace symbol on his forearm, symbolizing that he was never a part of the violence that was going on in his town, so close to his home, but he chose a different path, and the year 1991 on his knuckles, representing the year he was born.

On his left hand, the word "love" can be found on his knuckles, symbolizing again that love is the most important thing in the world. Recently, as we saw on social media, Roberto Firmino is getting a portrait of his beloved wife Larissa. Still, we don't know whereas of yet.

The last tattoo we will cover is the word "Deus" on his neck, meaning "God" in Portuguese, indicating that he is a man of faith.

TRENDSETTER

Apart from standing out on the pitch, Firmino also loves to stand out when it comes to his fashion sense.

He and his beautiful wife, who, as we mentioned, is a model and knows a thing or two about fashion, are known for their pictures while posing in flashy and extravagant outfits.

A family member who desired to remain anonymous revealed the following about the couple: *"Roberto and Larissa are similar — they love the good life, fast cars and comfortable homes. They are like David and Victoria Beckham. She is very body-conscious and likes keeping fit. They are really happy together and suit each other. She keeps him grounded, and she is very loyal."*

As Roberto Firmino remembers the times of his childhood, he once admitted that when he was a kid wandering the city centre, he would window-shop and tell his parents that he would be wearing all of those fashionable clothes and jewellery he would wear would see in the windows.

He visualized himself in that position. Roberto knew that one day he would be there. He never hoped it would happen; he never doubted it for a second. He never hoped it would happen; he never really doubted it either. He knew that when he became an adult, he would be a famous soccer player while at the same time taking care of his family. And just by wearing whatever clothes he wanted, without even thinking about things like that. This is the power of belief, and if you combine that with hard work, the world is yours.

Today, far from what he did when he was a boy, Firmino is known for wearing the latest brands, adopting the latest trends and even setting some trends on his own. No doubt that he worked hard for it, and he deserves to spoil himself once in a while.

Roberto is a happy guy, always with a smile on his face. But let's not forget that he had that smile even when he was poor. He was always happy and always looked on the bright side of things, keeping his head up.

When an interviewer asked the football star about his love for a luxury lifestyle, he replied: *"I like to try new things. Maybe I am a little vain. I have an exotic wardrobe. My style is flamboyant and bold when it comes to choosing what to wear. I search for different crazes on the internet, and either copy them or take what I want and make it my own style. I love edgy clothes. I am trying to create my own signature style, and I've been improving on it every day. It's about expressing who I am and finding out what suits me and what I like."*

STYLE OF PLAY

Now that we covered his fashion style and what makes him stand out, it's time to see what style he has on the pitch.

He primarily plays forward, but he could also occupy other positions, like winger, central midfielder, and attacking midfielder. He has an extraordinary ability to use his speed along with his close control to create chances.

Firmino is considered to be the most underrated number 9 in Europe. Let's see what it's all about.

Firmino is excellent at what he does, and he works harder than anyone out there, but his return from 21 league shots in two full seasons does not portray him as a reliable target threat.

Moreover, he "exceeded" his expected goals according to some famous websites that present reliable football statistics, with almost four goals.

Firmino is more than capable of getting out of tricky situations, meaning that he finds the back of the net with low-quality opportunities.

But Firmino is not just on the team to get the ball behind in the net, he is much more general, and much of what he does cannot be quantified. His assist against City was fifth in the Premier League and ninth in all competitions. Only when you include assistance do you realize how effective Firmino is as a striker who contributes to the team?

For context, Harry Kane was involved in 33 goals in all competitions, Romelu Lukaku was involved in 22, Morata in 16 and Sergio Agüero had 25 goals involved on his behalf. Firmino is 26 years old and spent time playing as a striker earlier in the season.

Football Whispers' data scientist Bobby Gardiner said that: "He is playing the role of Karim Benzema better than Benzema himself"

A selfless centre forward who allows widespread players to do what they do best.

Call Firmino whatever you want; you can call him a false nine. The truth is that he is a complete forward these days.

He holds the ball, wins his aerial duels, runs through the channels and runs behind the rival. His goal against City was one that we could expect Kane, Lukaku or Agüero to score.

He showed great movement to get to the Oxlade-Chamberlain pass, knocking John Stones out of the way before calmly tossing the ball over Ederson. It was an eerily quiet ending to what was a frantic soccer game. That was Firmino, the scorer. The first goal was to be Firmino, the creator. He fights Fabian Delph for the ball and gets it to Oxlade-Chamberlain. The former Arsenal player runs over Fernandinho before shooting past Ederson.

Not many other forwards in the Premier League try to get the ball back so tenaciously.

A former teammate that goes by the name of Ryan Babel describer himself as a "tricky player" while playing at Hoffenheim. He admitted that the Brazilian could dribble and shoot, having the ability to score from any angle or create an assist at any time.

And even though he was so talented and grabbed the headlines, he was very humble and didn't let the success go to his head.

Other important figures in the football world had to say this about the Brazilian wonder:

Arsene Wenger, the former Arsenal coach, expressed his admiration for Roberto Firmino, whom he considers unique. *"I like Salah very much, as do Mane. But don't forget an individual who sacrifices himself every game, Roberto Firmino. Just as Suarez did for Messi and Neymar, he is the player who works for the team's benefit and makes his teammates shine. It is the missing piece of a puzzle. It is very difficult to find a football player like Firmino "*, said the French technician.

Former footballer and pundit, Thierry Henry has said: "I'm enchanted by Roberto's (Firmino) style of play." He believes he is the only player playing like this in the world today. "He is a great football". It's incredible how smart he is in all the choices he makes; how technical he is, and how much he likes to work hard." *I think there are two more footballers in the world like him, but he doesn't want me to name them. I have seen footballers with a technique like Roberto Firmino, but combining attitude, intelligence and technique is exceptional. If you give Firmino the ball, he will score without difficulty. It's unique,"* said Thierry Henry.

Virgil van Dijk, the best defender and player of the last edition of the UEFA Champions League, said that he would have been afraid to have a direct opponent of Roberto Firmino: "He is a very important footballer for us." *As a central defender, I can say that he would have been a very difficult opponent, and I am happy because we are part of the same team. Roberto would be in big trouble for any defender in the world. He is a very good footballer ".*

PROFESSIONAL CAREER

We talked about what went on in Brazil and how he impressed the Germans while having bad luck with Marseille. But let's see what happened when he started his European adventure at Hoffenheim.

Firmino arrived at Hoffenheim in January 2011, in the middle of the season, his new club being on the 8th place in the Bundesliga ranking. But any hope of using it immediately disappeared when the results of the medical tests came.

Tanner recalls the moment: *"On arrival, we did a set of tests, and we couldn't believe it when we saw the results. They were so bad we had to redo them. With three matches a week and thousands of kilometres of travel, the Brazilian championship model had already made its mark. He was in a state of shock. "The new plan involved bringing Firmino to a suitable physical condition for the next season, part of this process being his use in the friendly matches of the U23 team, then coached by Markus*

Gisdol. "He played with us a few times, and I got to know him well," recalls Gisdol, now a coach in Cologne. *"He was weak and needed time to grow. German football requires a certain level of athletics, and he did not have it yet, but technically it was almost immediately obvious that he is a high-quality player. "*

To everyone's surprise, it took Firmino just a few weeks to get in good shape. With a stable situation in the middle of the standings, not having the pressure to qualify for the European Cups or relegation, Hoffenheim allowed himself to test it faster than everyone expected. *"We managed to develop his endurance and bring him into good physical condition very quickly,"* says Tanner, *"and he made his Bundesliga debut in February."*

Three goals in 11 matches (and a total of 470 minutes played) represented a solid performance in the given context, and Firmino continued with seven goals in his first full season. "Our style of play suited him," Tanner explains. *"We had fast transitions, and he is the kind of player who thrives in this system. He was also the perfect age, 19, in the process of learning.*

And in terms of personality, Firmino was the dream of any coach, a perfect professional. I didn't even need to motivate or criticize him." completes Gisdol.

For a young Brazilian ten thousand kilometres from home, the presence of compatriots was vital to facilitate integration, even if Luiz Gustavo left for Bayern after a short time. *"We had a Brazilian-German goalkeeping coach, Cesar Their, who took care of Roberto a lot. I also talked to him often about our experiences playing in Brazil,"* added Pfannenstiel, who joined the team a month after Firmino.

In the third season for Firmino, 2012-2013, Hoffenheim was close to relegation, but the one who saved them was Gisdol, named head coach in April after previously being the second coach at Schalke. His arrival had a major impact on the Brazilian's development in Germany. *"Already working with him at U23, I knew what to expect when I returned. He had already developed very well, but I wanted to help him take his game to the next level,"* says Gisdol. Firmino had an exceptional 2013-2014 season.

He scored 22 goals in all competitions and made 15 assists, culminating in his appointment as the season's revelation in the Bundesliga. *"It was just fantastic,"* Gisdol says proudly. *"He gave 100% every day, and when you are so focused and willing to work, your talent will grow exponentially. During that season, the results of the effort were seen. "*Pfannestiel agrees: *"I think he realized pretty quickly at Hoffenheim that talent will not be enough to succeed. Now I always say that Roberto has the qualities of a Brazilian and the mentality of a German. That's what makes him such a special player, and he discovered this combination at Hoffenheim. "*

He remained for the rest of the season at Hoffenheim, scoring seven goals and passing decisively 13 times. Still, a move to another level was inevitable. Liverpool paid 41 million euros in the summer of 2015. If there were any doubts about Firmino's arrival in Europe, they had disappeared before the next chapter of his career. "He was ready to play in the Premier League, no doubt," says Tanner. "You could see him grow from month to month, and he couldn't stay at Hoffenheim anymore. He had exceeded that level."

Liverpool was in full transformation after a 2014-2015 season ended in an unconvincing sixth place. After Firmino's first eight games at Anfield, Rodgers was sacked and replaced by Jurgen Klopp.

Paul Gorst of Liverpool Echo believes that the moment of change and the new manager was the perfect combination for Firmino. *"Those in charge of the transfers had seen Firmino as the target, even if Rodgers would have preferred Christian Benteke from Aston Villa. Eventually, they both made it to the club, but Rodgers couldn't find a place for Firmino - at one point, he ended up playing for Old Trafford. Klopp used him directly as a central striker. He liked Daniel Sturridge, but he got injured too often. Firmino was much more consistent from this point of view. This, combined with his defensive availability, made him an irreplaceable piece. "*

On November 21st, 2015, Liverpool, currently in 10th place, went to Manchester to face City for a difficult confrontation on the Etihad. In just 32 minutes, Liverpool was already 3-0, winning 4-1 in the end. *"Firmino scored the third goal and constantly harassed City's defence. It was brilliant and has grown steadily ever since,"* says Gorst.

The same thing happened with Liverpool under Klopp. Sadio Mané and Mohamed Salah completed the most devastating offensive trio in the Premier League, as shown by the 250 goals scored by the three at the beginning of the 2017-2018 season.

Unusual for a central striker, Firmino is easily overtaken by those who flank him, but that doesn't seem to matter. *"Firmino is the perfect binder for Salah and Mané,"* Gorst insists. *"The two have won the Golden Ice in recent seasons, but without Firmino, they would never have come close to those numbers. Liverpool fans would like to see more goals from him, but his goals are invariably what matters when he scores. "*

However, none of them was as decisive as the two scissors-kicks scored 13 years ago in the trials for Figueirense.
Tanner sees Firmino as one of the greatest achievements of his talent-hunting career, and that's not surprising. *We have contributed to the*

discovery of many players over the years, some of whom have even played for the German national team. But I have to say that Firmino is the best player I've discovered. You can never tell what the future holds when you look at a young player - you can imagine, but you have no certainty. Roberto is a good example of what you can achieve when you dedicate your body and soul to a goal."

As of lately, other clubs are interested in the talents that the Liverpool star possesses.

Bayern Munich is trying to strengthen its attack.

The German group wants to bring Roberto Firmino from Liverpool and Leroy Sane from Manchester City to strengthen the offensive compartment, announces The Sun.

Coach Hans Flick believes that Firmino is the perfect footballer to play in attack with Robert Lewandowski. The Brazilian is a basic man in Liverpool, but the English have great chances to bring Timo Werner from Leipzig. Bayern Munich is ready to offer 90 million euros for the Brazilian striker. This move could make Premier League leaders give up on Firmino.

Will Firmino leave Merseyside and embark on a new adventure by joining the German giants? We'll just have to wait and see, but one thing is for certain. Firmino will shine wherever he decides to play.

INTERNATIONAL CAREER

Roberto Firmino always dreamed of representing his country on the pitch. He knew that he could make a difference and enter Brazilian footballers' "fall of fame". But he had enormous shoes to fill.

Each of the five Brazilian teams that succeeded in winning the World Cup was special in its own way.

Selecao is probably the most talented team in the history of football. Everyone in the world knows it. If you ask 100 people about the memory, they have from the World Cup, there is a good chance that most of their answers will be in one direction. It's about the famous canary-yellow equipment, about the joy of football, it's about Selecao.

Brazil and the World Cup. World Cup and Brazil. What a symbiosis. No other nation has made its mark more than Brazilians in the entire history of the final world championship tournaments. Certainly, no other nation has had such an impact on the perception of football as Brazilians have.

And here comes a new team. A young, hungry team that needs to take their spot in history and Roberto Firmino is an important part of that team.

In October 2014, Firmino got the call. Yes, the call, asking him to join the national team. He was ecstatic. His dream was finally turning into reality. Wearing that yellow jersey and singing Brazil's national anthem on the pitch. He couldn't believe it, but he definitely earned it.

Firmino said: *"I am very happy to be nominated, and I would especially like to thank the team."*

Brazil has been fortunate enough to be blessed with some of the greatest strikers of all time. We're talking about the likes of Careca, Romario and Ronaldo, all of them earning a place in the country's hall of fame for their exploits in the final third.

They have, however, struggled to find Ronaldo's successor since his retirement in 2011.

Tremendously talented players like Alexandre Pato, Vagner Love, Fred and Luis Fabiano tried to fill those shoes. Unfortunately, they ended up failing to live up to the same high standards.

Due to his modest goalscoring record, Roberto Firmino has also faced plenty of criticism since taking up a highly coveted role in the team. However, he still has plenty of faith in his own ability. Asked if he wants to follow in the footsteps of Brazil's most revered strikers and forwards, the Liverpool star responded: *"Yes, definitely. I love playing in this position, and I want to be the player Brazil can rely on in this position."*

Firmino's defensive work has been a staple of his time at Anfield, but his coach at the national team wants his main focus to be getting on the end of attacks at a higher level, which he is now embracing. *"It's not that he asked me not to help out, but he wants me to always be in the area. I still have to get back to mark, but he wants me to chase back less after the ball, be in the box more,"* the 29-year-old said of his responsibilities for the Selecao. *"I have a natural urge to help out, get back – I do this for Liverpool – so I have to put this aside and do what Tite has asked of me. "I enjoy being involved in the play, creating goals, but I also enjoy being in the box, scoring goals."*

Firmino added after his team's victory over Bolivia: *"The performance of the whole team, the spirit we showed deserves congratulations. Getting off to a winning start was really important, and to do it with such a good performance makes it even better. "Scoring two goals was an incredible feeling. I had more chances, I could have scored more, but I'm very happy. I'm 29, and I feel I'm at the best moment of my career. "I want to keep working hard and help Selecao reach the World Cup."*

Roberto Firmino already had made his mark in his national team, and the stats speak for themselves.

The Brazilian star managed to get selected a total of 48 times for the national team, playing International Friendlies, World Cup Qualification matches, Copa America matches and of course, World Cup Matches.

In international games, he managed to score eight times while assisting two. At the same time, in World Cup qualification matches, the Brazilian found the net 4 times while assisting two times.

When it comes to Copa America, Firmino managed to bag 3 goals and the same number of assists, while in the world cup, he scored one time, but there will still be plenty of chances for the young forward.

CAREER STATS

We covered everything from his childhood when he used to play football without any shoes, but he never lost that fire and that drive that resided deep inside of him.

We took a look at his personal life, having a beautiful family alongside his wife Larissa and their two beautiful daughters. We talked about how he failed for Marseille but got accepted at Hoffenheim before becoming a real football superstar and joining Liverpool.

But how good is Roberto Firmino? We know that fellow players and some coaches praise the Brazilian, but their perspectives can be subjective. There's are a few things in this world that do not lie, and those are numbers. Statistics, to be exact. Let's see how many times Roberto Firmino managed to find the back of the net and how many times he participated in creating goals.

First off, we'll take a look at his Premier League stats. The place where he really showed signs that he could be one of the best footballers in the world and, why not, maybe win a Ballon d'Or one day.

In his 198 appearances for Liverpool, the forward managed to score an impressive 63 goals. In contrast, out of those appearances, 124 were wins and just 28 were losses. This goes to show how compact and creative is Liverpool's team.

Firmino manages to score 0.32 goals per match, which means a goal every three matches, which is quite impressive considering he is not exactly a striker.

Out of those 63 goals, 15 were headed, Firmino using his impressive condition and intelligence to position himself in the right spot at exactly the right time, not giving the defenders time to react.

Being a term of affection, Roberto, or "Bobby" as his teammates call him, can score with both of his feet, being quite successful no matter with which one he shoots. He scores a total of 32 goals using his right foot and another 15 with his left.

His accuracy is also lethal. Out of a total number of 474 shots fired towards the goal, 202 of them managed to hit the target. That's what we call a snipper's accuracy. And if we would convert that into a percentage, the number would translate into 43%.

And out of those shots, he got unlucky at times, or might we say that the goalkeeper got lucky, and he hit the woodwork a total of 12 times. We all know the feeling when that perfect shot has just the right speed and curve. As the ball is flying through the air, we can already see it going past the goalkeeper and hitting the net, but just at the last moment, it hits the woodwork, and you just can't believe it, all that's left for you to do is laugh it off and keep going.

When it comes to defence, Roberto is a well-disciplined player. He doesn't like to get involved in scuffles and avoids confrontation when he can. Out of the total of 220 fouls that he committed in his seasons at Liverpool, the Brazilian only receiver eight yellow cards and no red card. An impressive feat for any footballer.

Sometimes, when you're in the middle of a game and spirits are high, the score is even, you might get annoyed when an opposing player is rough and maybe grabs hold of your shirt, stopping you from advancing with the ball. But Roberto keeps his cool and plays by the rules, only focusing on the job he has to do, scoring goals and creating chances for his teammates.

We all know he's great when it comes to attacking. But what about the defensive part? Roberto Firmino says that he doesn't mind helping his midfielders or even his defenders if the situation calls for it. Brazilians have a reputation of attacking and being showmen, but he doesn't shy away from putting in the work, even when it comes to the defensive part of the game.

During his time at Liverpool so far, Roberto managed to block an impressive 136 shots and successfully tackled and won the ball a number of 278 times. This is how you know a player doesn't shy away from any aspect of the game.

He intercepted the ball 80 times and cleared it into safety a total of 67 times, while 50 of those being headed clearances, taking advantage of his height.

When it comes to the time he spent in the Bundesliga, even though he had fewer appearances than he has at Liverpool, Firmino managed to gather some impressive stats.

He stayed active and made 140 appearances for the German club Hoffenheim. Out of that time on the pitch, the Brazilian used his talents and managed to score 38 goals while being part of another 29 by assisting the player who put it in the back of the net.

When it comes to discipline, Firmino received 24 yellow cards, but, again, as he doesn't want to let his emotions get the better of him, he didn't receive a single red card over the course of his entire career in Germany.

Now let's talk about the Champions League. The biggest stage of all. Where Europe's best teams clash and fight for that beautiful trophy, each player was imagining they would have the chance to rise it above their head. At the same time, the infamous anthem plays in the background and confetti flying everywhere.

It's what every player from a European club dreams. It is the ultimate prize a team can get for their hard work and hours upon hours poured into training.

When it comes to how well Roberto Firmino did in the Champions League, we can start off by saying that the first time he played in the competition was in 2017/2018.

He had 13 appearances, as long as two appearances in the qualifiers, where he managed to score an impressive number of 10 goals in the main competition and 1 in the qualifying round. Apart from finding the back of the net ten times, the number 9 also provided eight assists.

He accumulated just two yellow cards with no red card insight, as usual when it comes to yellow cards.

Unfortunately for Liverpool and their striker, Firmino, even if they had an amazing season and eliminated teams like Portuguese giants Porto and Roma, the Merseyside team reached the final and faced Real Madrid. While it is difficult to say if they would have been able to defeat the Spanish squad, it is worth noting that even with a fantastic season, eliminating Porto and Roma from their way to the final wasn't enough.

The game was close, up until the second half. Both teams had an almost equal number of shots. The Spanish giants managed to shoot 14 times while Liverpool did it for 13 times, but only two shots were on target. Apart from that close statistic, Real Madrid we're clearly the better team. Their possession of the ball was 66% opposed to Liverpool's 34%.

Firmino's team completed 327 successful passes while the team from Madrid managed a whopping 645. The English side was also more aggressive, committing 18 fouls opposed to 5 fouls to form Real.

Hopes were up for Liverpool fans. They already imagined their team lifting the trophy above their heads and bringing it to Liverpool.

But then, disaster struck. Karim Benzema managed to score the first goal of the final after 51 minutes of playtime while being closely followed by Liverpool's Sadio Mane, who found the net in the 55th minute.

Gareth Bale achieved the impossible and scored in the 64th minute. At the same time, the final blow that crushed Firmino's dreams came in the 83rd minute, after a headed effort.

The dream was gone. At the moment, at least. Because next year, it was going to be different. In the 2018/2019 season, Firmino managed to score a total of 4 goals and assist one time in his four appearances in the Champions League.

Even though the stats don't seem that impressive, he was still an important part of the puzzle, which led Liverpool to glory.

It was from Liverpool against Barcelona. After eliminating teams like Bayern, the feared German giants with the aggregate score being 3-1, next came Porto, again then the biggest surprise of the tournament. The Catalan team managed to get three past Liverpool's goalkeepers in the first leg while also maintaining a clean sheet. It was 3-0 after the first leg, and no one would give Liverpool a chance. But back home, things changed.

The players had enough and knew it was time to turn things up. During an exciting game, where Liverpool had only seven shots towards goal and only three on target, all of those precise shots found the net. And with the help from Mascherano's own goal, Liverpool managed to get the win in the 93rd minute, eliminating one of the most feared teams in Europe.

Now, one more step to the cup and eternal glory. Liverpool would face English rivals Tottenham in the final. Another surprise.

The game was close with plenty of drama, but in the end, Liverpool managed to take it home, scoring the second goal in the 87th minute, making it 0-2 for Merseyside.

The long journey was over. The Champions League trophy was theirs.

This is the first time Roberto Firmino could say that he was part of the best team in Europe.

When it comes to other trophies, the Brazilian didn't shy away from the winning side. From the total of 5 trophies that he won, 4 of them was at club level, with Liverpool.

But let's start with the international trophy. In 2018/2019, Firmino managed to win the Copa America with Brazil, having an integral part in the outcome.

That same year, as we said before, the Brazilian got his hands on that coveted Champions League trophy followed by the UEFA SUPERCUP.

After that, he won the Premier League with the Merseyside team as well as the FIFA Club World Cup.

The last years have been filled with successes for the Brazilian forward, and he owes it all to his parents. Firmino is close to his family and believes that if it hadn't been for them, he would not have achieved so much in life, and for this, he made sure that they wouldn't have to worry about anything ever again.

What will be next to the famous number 9? Will he spread his wings and fly off to Germany, but this time joining Bayern Munchen? Or will he stay at Liverpool under Klopp and continue making history for the legendary English side?

Only time will tell, but one thing is certain. Firmino's talents are welcomed at any top club in Europe.

Bonus Page

Free Word Search
Liverpool's Legends

FORMER 1990-2000 (1)

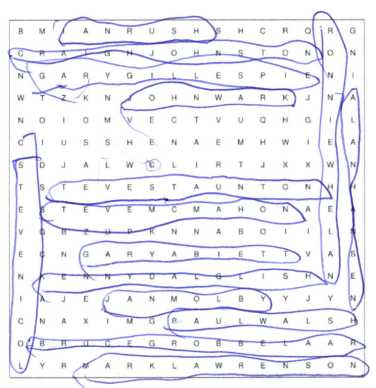

IAN RUSH JAN MOLBY GARY GILLESPIE STEVE NICOL PAUL WALSH
BRUCE GROBBELAAR RONNIE WHELAN STEVE MCMAHON STEVE STAUNTON ALAN HANSEN
KENNY DALGLISH JOHN WARK GARY ABLETT MARK LAWRENSON CRAIGH JOHNSTON

FORMER 1990-2000 (2)

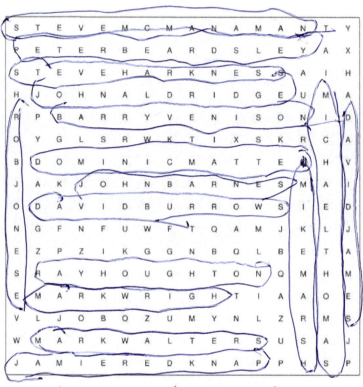

FORMER 1970-1980

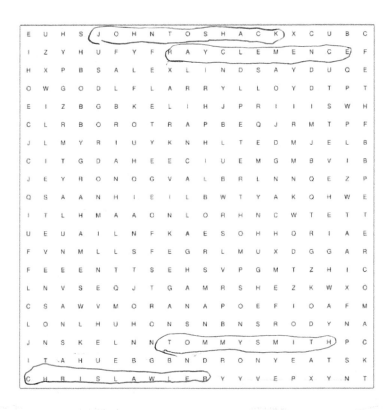

IAN ST JOHN	CHRIS LAWLER	IAN CALLAGHAN	WILLIE STEVENSON	GEOFF STRONG
RON YEATS	PETER THOMPSON	BOBBY GRAHAM	TOMMY SMITH	GORDON MILNE
EMLYN HUGHES	ALEX LINDSAY	PHIL BOERSMA	STEVE HEIGHWAY	BRIAN HALL
RAY CLEMENCE	LARRY LLOYD	ALUN EVANS	KEVIN KEEGAN	PETER COMACK
JOHN TOSHACK				

FORMER 1980-1990

G	A	I	S	Z	J	G	D	I	Z	S	H	S	T	Z	J
S	Z	S	R	M	I	R	A	A	H	D	A	X	R	H	E
P	C	P	K	S	M	A	V	D	C	A	W	B	Q	X	T
J	I	D	P	E	M	E	I	Q	J	V	K	U	I	I	A
X	P	J	H	N	Y	M	D	I	V	I	X	E	J	H	L
H	R	D	I	J	C	E	F	F	I	D	L	B	O	J	A
Z	A	F	L	S	A	S	A	F	G	J	O	H	E	Q	N
C	Y	K	T	S	S	O	I	L	Z	O	S	M	Y	V	K
Z	K	K	H	A	E	U	R	K	I	H	Y	Z	J	P	E
J	E	L	O	M	L	N	C	M	S	N	W	A	O	H	N
B	N	S	M	M	Y	E	L	A	D	S	H	K	N	I	N
P	N	Q	P	Y	X	S	O	I	S	O	L	U	E	L	E
Z	E	X	S	L	N	S	U	Y	K	N	Q	B	S	N	D
J	D	C	O	E	C	Z	G	J	V	P	V	L	B	E	Y
O	Y	E	N	E	E	D	H	I	M	Q	G	O	M	A	K
O	T	E	R	R	Y	M	C	D	E	M	O	T	T	L	K

JOEY JONES   SAMMY LEE   DAVID JOHNSON   GRAEME SOUNESS

TERRY MCDEMOTT   ALAN KENNEDY   PHIL THOMPSON   DAVID FAIRCLOUGH

JIMMY CASE   RAY KENNEDY   PHIL NEAL

FORMER 1940-1960

P	R	R	J	S	C	O	J	I	M	H	A	R	L	E	Y
K	M	A	T	T	B	U	S	B	Y	F	D	C	I	Y	O
N	B	K	V	U	J	B	J	L	C	H	X	C	L	C	C
N	R	N	K	B	I	L	L	Y	L	I	D	E	L	X	H
M	I	C	Z	H	J	A	C	K	B	A	L	M	E	R	O
B	A	Y	R	A	Y	L	A	M	B	E	R	T	N	O	H
O	N	R	T	Y	C	J	I	M	M	Y	P	A	Y	N	E
B	J	I	K	E	V	I	N	B	A	R	O	N	W	H	C
P	A	L	G	J	E	D	D	I	E	S	P	I	C	E	R
A	C	D	T	U	L	F	B	I	L	L	J	O	N	E	S
I	K	O	H	P	H	I	L	T	A	Y	L	O	R	H	E
S	S	N	A	L	B	E	R	S	T	U	B	B	I	N	S
L	O	E	L	A	U	R	I	E	H	U	G	H	E	S	W
E	N	C	Y	R	I	L	S	I	D	L	O	W	O	K	H
Y	W	R	H	Y	T	S	F	F	Q	N	B	G	F	K	M
Z	M	V	W	I	L	L	I	E	F	A	G	A	N	W	X

LAURIE HUGHES	BILL JONES	KEVIN BARON	EDDIE SPICER	ALBER STUBBINS
JIM HARLEY	MATT BUSBY	BOB PAISLEY	JACK BALMER	PHIL TAYLOR
CYRIL SIDLOW	BILLY LIDEL	CYRIL DONE	BRIAN JACKSON	WILLIE FAGAN
JIMMY PAYNE	RAY LAMBERT			

FORMER 1960-1970

I	M	V	T	O	B	E	R	T	S	L	A	T	E	R	I
G	F	S	C	D	W	J	I	M	M	Y	M	E	L	I	A
E	W	Z	A	L	A	N	A	C	O	U	R	T	N	D	W
O	G	N	A	L	O	U	I	S	B	I	M	P	S	O	N
F	H	A	K	G	E	R	R	Y	B	Y	R	N	E	D	R
F	G	R	O	Y	S	A	U	N	D	E	R	S	O	I	O
T	G	T	O	M	M	Y	Y	O	U	N	G	E	R	C	N
W	T	O	M	M	Y	L	E	I	S	H	M	A	N	K	N
E	T	O	M	M	Y	L	A	W	R	E	N	C	E	W	I
N	I	N	R	I	D	E	E	T	B	V	G	X	B	H	E
T	H	U	C	N	R	O	G	E	R	H	U	N	T	I	M
Y	J	I	M	M	Y	H	A	R	R	O	W	E	R	T	O
M	I	V	H	L	G	E	P	G	Y	H	S	X	C	E	R
A	Y	J	O	H	N	N	Y	W	H	E	E	L	E	R	A
N	V	G	W	N	O	J	O	H	N	E	V	A	N	S	N
W	J	O	H	N	M	O	L	Y	N	E	U	X	V	W	V

JIMMY HARROWER	JOHN EVANS	JOHNNY WHEELER	LOUIS BIMPSON	TOMMY LAWRENCE
BERT SLATER	ROY SAUNDERS	JOHN MOLYNEUX	JIMMY MELIA	ALAN ACOURT
GERRY BYRNE	GEOFF TWENTYMAN	ROGER HUNT	TOMMY LEISHMAN	DICK WHITE
TOMMY YOUNGER	RONNIE MORAN			

FORMER 1920-1940

H	F	E	S	W	A	D	S	W	O	R	T	H	W	L	T
A	X	D	J	A	C	K	I	E	P	V	V	K	G	U	C
R	W	M	P	B	J	T	L	W	P	T	B	G	U	L	U
R	X	E	L	A	U	H	O	J	A	C	K	S	O	N	M
Y	S	D	B	S	J	L	K	A	M	S	D	N	C	G	T
S	L	H	A	X	I	W	A	L	T	E	R	T	H	B	G
Y	H	C	L	M	J	D	N	N	N	W	F	O	A	W	O
D	U	E	O	C	M	U	I	K	M	Q	R	M	M	H	R
L	I	R	L	T	L	C	Y	C	Y	I	E	M	B	O	D
U	B	C	S	D	J	R	N	A	K	A	D	Y	E	P	O
H	H	P	K	U	O	O	I	A	X	A	R	D	R	K	N
F	E	S	C	V	W	N	C	L	B	A	A	T	S	I	D
S	O	L	A	F	W	J	E	K	E	V	U	Z	H	N	N
B	S	A	H	O	D	G	S	O	N	Y	T	O	M	U	U
T	Y	J	A	M	E	S	H	V	T	O	X	C	C	C	R
R	B	V	S	I	Y	X	V	F	O	R	S	H	A	W	F

TOMMY	LUCAS	FRED	HOPKIN	DICK
EDMED	TOM	BROMILOW	HARRY	CHAMBERS
JACKIE	SHELDON	JAMES	JACKSON	ARTHUR
RILEY	JOCK	MCNAB	DICK	FORSHAW
WALTER	WADSWORTH	GORDON	HODGSON	

FORMER 1910-1920

V	E	G	I	I	T	Y	D	O	F	P	D	F	E	I	G
A	Q	N	R	R	R	R	Y	G	O	A	M	T	O	M	J
P	E	L	E	J	O	B	H	B	R	A	D	L	E	Y	W
P	U	B	A	F	M	I	F	E	R	G	U	S	O	N	Y
G	O	R	W	C	Y	L	Q	L	R	C	I	B	J	P	M
R	C	A	S	R	E	L	M	O	D	H	R	R	A	G	A
E	R	W	R	E	P	Y	I	N	J	O	O	R	M	D	Y
C	P	A	V	M	L	H	L	G	A	R	B	O	E	Q	W
J	H	H	M	B	E	L	L	W	M	L	E	N	S	J	N
W	B	O	R	W	O	G	E	O	E	T	R	A	T	K	X
X	T	L	O	A	H	B	R	R	S	O	T	L	R	E	E
C	X	L	F	G	I	P	K	T	Y	N	S	R	L	N	L
S	C	O	T	T	M	M	W	H	S	B	O	E	O	W	I
T	H	A	R	D	Y	M	A	C	K	I	N	L	A	Y	S
Q	D	O	N	A	L	D	F	G	H	A	R	R	O	P	H
Y	C	C	A	M	P	B	E	L	L	M	S	A	M	T	A

EPHRAIM	LONGWORTH	KEN	CAMPBELL	ROBERT
CRAWFORD	BILL	LACEY	HARRY	LOWE
BOB	PURSELL	ELISHA	SCOTT	DONALD
MACKINLAY	JAMES	HARROP	RONAL	ORR
JAMES	BRADLEY	TOM	MILLER	TOM
CHORLTON	SAM	HARDY	ROBERT	FERGUSON

FORMER 1899-1910

V	R	O	B	I	N	S	O	N	A	C	I
L	H	E	W	I	T	T	P	A	R	R	Y
P	E	R	K	I	N	S	E	I	T	G	X
M	A	U	R	I	C	E	K	Q	H	O	R
W	L	R	G	R	J	A	C	K	U	L	A
A	E	M	K	G	O	D	D	A	R	D	I
L	X	S	T	I	H	B	I	L	L	I	S
K	M	A	T	N	N	N	B	K	B	E	B
E	E	M	J	O	E	S	C	I	I	X	E
R	A	Z	L	R	M	A	O	J	E	H	C
P	F	J	W	I	J	L	X	N	W	N	K
X	I	S	E	Q	M	F	T	F	Z	G	N

ROBBIE	ROBINSON	JACK	COX	ALEX
RAISBECK	ALF	WEST	JOE	HEWITT
ARTHUR	GODDARD	TOM	JOHN	WALKER
JACK	PARKINSON	SAM	GOLDIE	MAURICE
PARRY	BILL	PERKINS		

FORMER 1899-1910

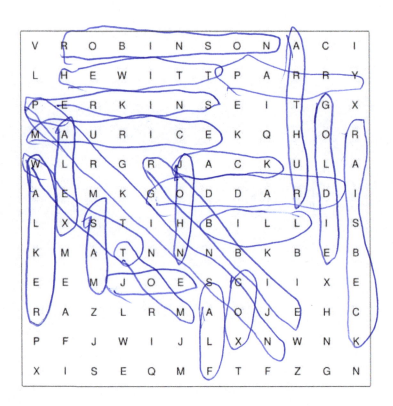

Printed in Great Britain
by Amazon